Remember me when you do pray,
that hope doth lead from day to day
anne boleyn

The
Anne Boleyn Files
Tudor Calendar 2023

The Anne Boleyn Files Tudor Calendar

Copyright © 2022
MadeGlobal Publishing

ISBN-13: 978-84-125953-1-4

M

MadeGlobal Publishing

For more information on
MadeGlobal Publishing, visit our website:
www.madeglobal.com

Welcome to the Anne Boleyn Files Tudor Calendar 2023! It's good to be back after having a break during the pandemic.

Our calendar is a celebration of all things Tudor and is the result of our annual photography competition. It comprises photos taken by Anne Boleyn Files followers of Tudor-related things, whether they're places, objects, or re-enactments.

This year, our calendar features the Tower of London, Eltham Palace, Rievaulx Abbey, Hever Castle, Little Moreton Hall and Hampton Court Palace, and Anne Boleyn's famous inscription, an Anne Boleyn re-enactor, and a cross-stitch. There is something to enjoy every month.

A big thank you to Ian Rotondi, Dawn Sampays, Susan Abernethy, Vicky West, Debra Glass, Elizabeth Redhead, Elaine Louise Ryan, Alison Cullen, Jane Desilet, Charlotte Huffington-Shinn, and Nikki Cox for their photos, and congratulations to Jane, who is the overall winner and whose photo is featured on the cover.

Have a wonderful 2023!

Claire Ridgway

January

Sunday	Monday	Tuesday	Wednesday	Thursday	Friday	Saturday
1	2	3	4	5	6	7
8	9	10	11	12	13	14 *1536: Death of Catherine of Aragon*
15 *1559: Coronation of Elizabeth I*	16	17	18 *1486: Marriage of Henry VII & Elizabeth of York*	19	20	21
22	23	24	25 *1533: Marriage of Henry VIII & Anne Boleyn*	26	27	28 *1457: Birth of Henry VII* *1547: Death of Henry VIII, accession of Edward VI*
29	30	31	1	2	3	4

A stunning view of the Tower of London by
Ian Rotondi, showing its many towers.

FEBRUARY

Sunday	Monday	Tuesday	Wednesday	Thursday	Friday	Saturday
29	30	31	1	2	3	4
5	6	7	8	9	10	11
12	13	14	15 *1587: Execution of Mary, Queen of Scots*	16	17	18 *1466: Birth of Elizabeth of York* *1503: Death of Elizabeth of York*
19 *1554: Executions of Lady Jane Grey & Lord Guildford Dudley*	20 *1542: Execution of Catherine Howard*	21	22	23	24	25 *1516: Birth of Mary I*
26	27 *1547: Coronation of Edward VI*	28	1	2	3	4

We loved *Dawn Sampays'* quirky photo showing the words that Anne Boleyn wrote in her book of hours with the grounds of Hever Castle in the background.

MARCH

Sunday	Monday	Tuesday	Wednesday	Thursday	Friday	Saturday
26	27	28	1	2	3	4
5	6	7	8	9	10	11
12	13	14	15	16	17	18
19	20	21	22	23	24	25 *1496: Birth of Mary Tudor, Queen of France*
26	27	28	29	30	31 *1603: Death of Elizabeth I, accession of James I*	1

This impressive photo by *Susan Abernethy* is of the Great Hall of Eltham Palace, the location of the nursery of Henry VII and Elizabeth of York's children.

April

Sunday	Monday	Tuesday	Wednesday	Thursday	Friday	Saturday
26	27	28	29	30	31	1
2	3	4	5	6	7	8
1502: Death of Arthur Tudor, Prince of Wales						
9	10	11	12	13	14	15
16	17	18	19	20	21	22
23	24	25	26	27	28	29
					1509: Death of Henry VII, accession of Henry VIII	
30	1	2	3	4	5	6

We're always impressed by the beauty of the monasteries dissolved during Henry VIII's reign, but also touched by sadness too. *Vicky West's photo is of Rievaulx Abbey.*

MAY

Sunday	Monday	Tuesday	Wednesday	Thursday	Friday	Saturday
30	1	2	3	4	5	6
7	8	9	10	11	12	13
14	15	16	17	18	19 *1536: Execution of Anne Boleyn*	20
21	22	23	24	25	26	27
28	29	30 *1536: Marriage of Henry VIII & Jane Seymour*	31	1	2	3

Here's a lovely photo by *Debra Glass* starring Belle Johnston as Anne Boleyn.

Jane Seymour

Anne Boleyn

Anne of Cleves

Catherine Howard

Catherine of Aragon

Catherine Parr

ELR

JUNE

Sunday	Monday	Tuesday	Wednesday	Thursday	Friday	Saturday
28	29	30	31	1	2	3
4	5	6	7	8	9	10
11 *1509: Marriage of Henry VIII & Catherine of Aragon*	12	13	14	15	16	17
18	19	20	21	22	23	24 *1509: Coronation of Henry VIII & Catherine of Aragon*
25 *1533: Death of Mary Tudor, Queen of France*	26	27	28 *1491: Birth of Henry VIII*	29	30	1

1533: Coronation of Anne Boleyn (Thursday 1)

Many hours of work have gone into *Elizabeth Redhead's* cross-stitch of Henry VIII and his six wives.

July

Sunday	Monday	Tuesday	Wednesday	Thursday	Friday	Saturday
25	26	27	28	29	30	1
2	3	4	5	6	7	8
9	10	11	12	13 *1543: Marriage of Henry VIII & Catherine Parr*	14	15 *1553: Death of Edward VI, accession of Lady Jane Grey*
16	17	18	19 *1553: Mary I proclaimed queen*	20	21	22
23 *1557: Death of Anne of Cleves*	24	25 *1554: Marriage of Mary I & Philip of Spain*	26	27	28 *1540: Marriage of Henry VIII & Catherine Howard*	29
30	31	1	2	3	4	5

Here's *Elaine Louise Ryan's* pretty photo of the Tudor Garden at Hever Castle, with the castle shown in the background.

August

Sunday	Monday	Tuesday	Wednesday	Thursday	Friday	Saturday
30	31	1	2	3	4	5
6	7	8	9	10	11	12
13	14	15	16	17	18	19
20	21	22	23	24	25	26
27	28	29 *1485: Battle of Bosworth*	30	31	1	2

Both quirky and miraculous, and even a little bit magical, we love *Alison Cullen's* photo of Little Moreton Hall.

SEPTEMBER

Sunday	Monday	Tuesday	Wednesday	Thursday	Friday	Saturday
27	28	29	30	31	1	2
3	4	5	6	7	8	9
10	11	12 *1548: Death of Catherine Parr*	13	14	15	16
17	18	19	20	21	22	23
24	25	26	27 *1486: Birth of Arthur Tudor, Prince of Wales*	28	29	30

Jane Desilet's photo looking back at Hever Castle across the river takes us back to the time of the Tudors.

OCTOBER

Sunday	Monday	Tuesday	Wednesday	Thursday	Friday	Saturday
1	2	3	4	5	6	7
8 *1553: Coronation of Mary I*	9	10	11	12	13	14
15	16	17	18 *1541: Death of Margaret Tudor, Queen of Scotland*	19 *1537: Birth of Edward VI*	20	21
22	23	24 *1537: Death of Jane Seymour*	25	26	27	28
29	30 *1485: Coronation of Henry VII*	31	1	2	3	4

Hampton Court Palace still has a wealth of Tudor decorations to see. *Charlotte Huffington-Shinn* has taken a picture of the inside of an entrance arch.

November

Sunday	Monday	Tuesday	Wednesday	Thursday	Friday	Saturday
29	30	31	1	2	3	4
5	6	7	8	9	10	11
12	13	14	15	16	17 *1558: Death of Mary I, accession of Elizabeth I*	18
19	20	21	22	23	24	25 *1487: Coronation of Elizabeth of York*
26	27	28 *1489: Birth of Margaret Tudor, Queen of Scotland*	29	30	1	2

Hever Castle is a firm favourite as it is so beautiful all year round, but never more so than *Nikki Cox's* photo taken in the "golden hour" as the sun goes down.

DECEMBER

Sunday	Monday	Tuesday	Wednesday	Thursday	Friday	Saturday
26	27	28	29	30	1	2
3	4	5	6	7	8	9
10	11	12	13	14	15 *1542: Birth of Mary, Queen of Scots*	16
17	18	19	20	21	22	23 *1485: Birth of Catherine of Aragon*
24	25	26	27	28	29	30
31	1	2	3	4	5	6

As the year comes to an end, what better than the hearty setting of Hampton Court Palace Kitchens taken by *Ian Rotondi?*

The Anne Boleyn Files Creator

Claire Ridgway is the author of the best-selling books: *George Boleyn: Tudor Poet, Courtier and Dipomat* (co-written with Clare Cherry), *On This Day in Tudor History*, *The Fall of Anne Boleyn: A Countdown*, *The Anne Boleyn Collection* and *The Anne Boleyn Collection II*, *Sweating Sickness in a Nutshell*, *Tudor Places of Great Britain*, *Illustrated Kings and Queen of England*, *The Life of Anne Boleyn Colouring Book* and *On This Day in Tudor History II*. Claire is the historical oracle (her best friend called her that so she's going with it) behind The Anne Boleyn Files history website, which is known for its historical accuracy. Claire's mission is to get to the truth behind Anne Boleyn's story and to share that with everyone. Claire is also the founder of the Tudor Society, an online hub connecting Tudor history lovers, historians and authors from all over the world, and the woman behind the popular Anne Boleyn Files and Tudor Society YouTube Channel - you could say that Claire is a bit of a Tudor nut!

Books by Claire Ridgway

The Anne Boleyn Collection:
The Real Truth About the Tudors

The Anne Boleyn Collection II:
Anne Boleyn and the Boleyn Family

The Anne Boleyn Collection III:
Celebrating Ten Years of TheAnneBoleynFiles

The Fall of Anne Boleyn:
A Countdown

George Boleyn:
Tudor Poet, Courtier & Diplomat (with Clare Cherry)

Illustrated Kings and Queens of England

Tudor Places of Great Britain

Sweating Sickness: In a Nutshell

On This Day in Tudor History

On This Day in Tudor History II

The Life of Anne Boleyn Colouring Book

Lightning Source UK Ltd.
Milton Keynes UK
UKHW050634091222
413634UK00002B/167